Teen Pregnancy and Motherhood

A YOUNG WOMAN'S GUIDE
TO CONTEMPORARY ISSUES™

Teen Pregnancy and Motherhood

MARY-LANE KAMBERG

ROSEN
PUBLISHING®

New York

For Rebekka

Published in 2013 by The Rosen Publishing Group, Inc.
29 East 21st Street, New York, NY 10010

Library of Congress Cataloging-in-Publication Data

Kamberg, Mary-Lane, 1948–
Teen pregnancy and motherhood/Mary-Lane Kamberg. — 1st ed.
    p. cm. — (A young woman's guide to contemporary issues)
Includes bibliographical references and index.
ISBN 978-1-4488-8397-4 (library binding)
1. Teenage pregnancy—Juvenile literature. 2. Motherhood—Juvenile literature. 3. Newborn infants—Care. I. Title.
RG556.5.K36 2013
618.200835—dc23

                                                                2012016559

Manufactured in the United States of America

CPSIA Compliance Information: Batch #W12YA. For further information, contact Rosen Publishing, New York, New York, at 1-800-237-9932.

Contents

Introduction 6

1 Conception and Choices 10

2 Preparation for Childbirth 25

3 Your Pregnancy 40

4 Getting Equipped for Motherhood and Baby Care 52

5 Having Your Baby 65

6 Why Babies Cry 75

7 Baby Care and Safety 84

Glossary 96

For More Information 98

For Further Reading 103

Bibliography 105

Index 108

INTRODUCTION

If you're a pregnant teen, you're not alone. About one million teenagers in the United States annually become pregnant, according to the Centers for Disease Control and Prevention (CDC). Research suggests that approximately 50 percent of adolescent pregnancies occur within the first six months of intercourse. Of those pregnancies, about 95 percent are unplanned.

The Alan Guttmacher Institute, a nonprofit non-partisan research group in New York, studied teens in Canada, France, Great Britain, Sweden, and the United States. Even though American teens engage in sexual activity at about the same rate as teens in other Western countries, the U.S. teen pregnancy rate is higher. Researchers think there are several reasons for this. Americans use contraception less often and have more limited access to health care services than their counterparts in other developed countries. The study found that only about 40 percent of American teens use oral contraceptives compared to 70 percent of other Western teens.

Of course, statistics don't much matter if you're one of the young women who find out they're pregnant. Upon learning of a pregnancy—

and confirming it with a blood test and pelvic exam by a health care provider—a teen faces a number of choices. Will she have the baby and take care of him or her? Put the baby up for adoption? Find a foster parent for the first several months or years? Raise the child in the grandparents' home? Or have an abortion? In the United States, about 51 percent of adolescent mothers decide to have the baby, 35 percent choose to have an abortion, and 14 percent of the pregnancies end in miscarriage or stillbirth. If you decide to keep your baby, you'll need lots of accurate information and a reliable support system.

Keeping a baby is a lifelong responsibility. It takes dedication, patience, and commitment. Teens who choose to keep their babies face more challenges than older mothers, including social stigma, poverty, and school absences. But with proper education, practice, and family or community support, teenagers can be good parents.

The first concern is the pregnancy itself. Getting prenatal medical care is important. So is good nutrition. The idea that you're eating for two is true—not in quantity but in quality. The developing baby eats what you eat. You'll want to follow a diet that has the nutrients he or she needs. (Keep in mind that the stuff you're supposed to eat—and avoid—is good for you, too.)

You'll want to learn about what pregnancy does to your own body, as well as how the baby grows over the approximately nine months of gestation. You'll benefit from childbirth education that includes a list of options about labor, delivery, and birth, and you'll want to prepare for bringing the baby home. What kind of crib, car seat, and other items do you need? What about clothing for the newborn?

Other preparations include what and how you will feed the baby. Will you breastfeed? Use formula? Do you know how to bathe an infant? How much sleep does a baby need? And how can you keep the baby safe?

Being a parent is a big job, but it also has significant rewards. Arm yourself with as much information as you can. Ask for help when you need it.

Welcome to motherhood.

UNPLANNED
PARENTHOOD
SAFE SEX
MOTHERHOOD
BIRTH PLAN
single mom
Pregnancy
TEEN
Childbirth
CONCEPTION

CHAPTER 1

CONCEPTION AND CHOICES

If you are sexually active, there is always a chance that you'll become pregnant, even if you're practicing "safe" sex. Condoms to prevent pregnancy and sexually transmitted infections, as well as other forms of contraception, can fail.

For example, according to Contracept.org, an organization that provides up-to-date information on sex-related issues, avoiding sexual intercourse near the time of ovulation (when pregnancy is most likely) has up to a 25 percent failure rate during the first year of use. Male condoms have a 15 percent failure rate, and oral hormone pills have an 8 percent failure rate over the same time. Other forms of pregnancy prevention, such as the pullout method, are unreliable at a 27 percent failure rate. Of course, the lowest pregnancy rate (zero) comes from complete abstinence. The highest comes from unprotected sex.

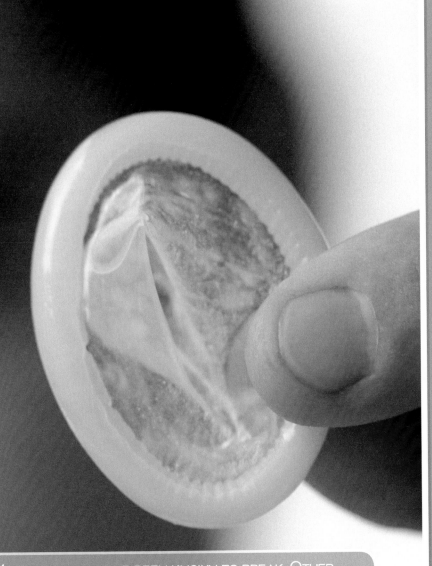

MALE CONDOMS HAVE BEEN KNOWN TO BREAK. OTHER FORMS OF CONTRACEPTION ALSO FAIL AT TIMES. COMPLETE ABSTINENCE FROM SEXUAL INTERCOURSE IS THE ONLY RELIABLE WAY TO AVOID PREGNANCY.

AM I PREGNANT?

Conception usually occurs within twenty-four hours of ovulation, the time the ovary releases a mature egg. Fertilization occurs when sperm released by the male during sex penetrates the egg.

The fertilized egg is called a zygote. Within the first twenty-four hours, cells begin to divide. The developing baby is called an embryo until the eighth week of growth. After that, it is called a fetus.

Beginning at conception, the mother's body produces a hormone called human chorionic gonadotropin (HCG). HCG is a pregnancy hormone present in the blood. About three days after conception, the embryo attaches to the lining of the uterus and continues to grow. The uterus is a hollow, pear-shaped organ in a female's lower abdomen. Some women experience slight

bleeding, called spotting, for a day or two when implantation occurs.

Some mothers say they "knew" the exact moment they became pregnant. Others identify certain symptoms within one week of conception. Still others don't suspect pregnancy or notice any symptoms for two or more weeks. Every woman's experience is different. And every pregnancy is different, even for the same woman.

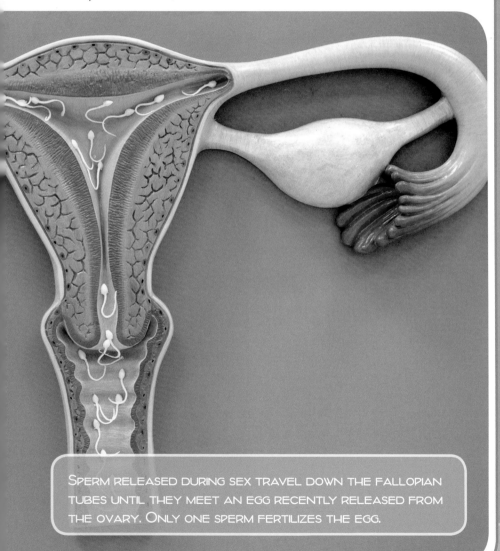

SPERM RELEASED DURING SEX TRAVEL DOWN THE FALLOPIAN TUBES UNTIL THEY MEET AN EGG RECENTLY RELEASED FROM THE OVARY. ONLY ONE SPERM FERTILIZES THE EGG.

PREGNANCY SYMPTOMS

Early signs of pregnancy include a missed menstrual period (or only a brief, light period), tender or swollen breasts, nausea or vomiting ("morning sickness"), fatigue, frequent urination, and mood swings. If you have missed a period and have any or many of these symptoms, you may want to take a home pregnancy test. These are available at any drugstore and can be quite reliable even early in a pregnancy. However, it may take two or three weeks after fertilization for the hormone to occur in high enough amounts to be detected.

Home pregnancy tests look for the presence of HCG in the urine. The hormone is present only if you are pregnant or have recently given birth or had a miscarriage. Home tests are about 97 percent accurate, according to WebMD. You can increase the accuracy of the result by checking the expiration date on the package and carefully following the directions. The best time of day to test is the first urination of the day when the urine is more concentrated.

Some medications can cause positive results in women who are not pregnant. Avoid aspirin at least twenty-four

WHEN YOU LEARN YOU'RE PREGNANT, START BUILDING A SUPPORT SYSTEM. IN MOST CASES A PARENT IS THE BEST PERSON TO TELL FIRST, BUT YOU CAN GET HELP FROM OTHER ADULTS.

hours before testing. If you're taking tranquilizers or anti-convulsants, you can also get a false-positive result. On the other hand, diuretics or antihistamines may give a negative reading even if you really are pregnant.

If the home test is positive—or if it's negative but you think you really might be pregnant—seek confirmation from a health care provider. You'll get another type of pregnancy test that is typically done in a medical lab, doctor's office, or clinic. It also tests for HCG, but it looks for the hormone in the blood. The health care provider will also perform a pelvic exam to confirm the pregnancy and gauge the size of the uterus.

It's Positive. Now What?

Don't think you can handle this situation alone. You can't keep your condition secret for long. Telling your parents may be difficult, but if you can talk to them, they can help you decide what to do.

Another choice is a pregnancy option counselor. You can talk to

With today's technology and social media, rumors fly at the speed of light. If you become pregnant, try to have a plan in place before telling friends.

a counselor without parental consent, even if you're younger than eighteen. But if you want to include parents or the baby's father, that's all right, too. The counselor will help you make your own decisions based on accurate information about available alternatives. You might also confide in a trusted relative, teacher, or clergyperson. If you want to keep your condition quiet until you've made a final decision, be careful about sharing the news with

friends. Gossip spreads fast, especially with the use of social media.

Is Marriage a Good Idea?

Forty or fifty years ago, the term "shotgun wedding" referred to a marriage that occurred because the young woman was pregnant "out of wedlock." Social norms included a stigma about sexual intercourse outside of marriage. The stigma also applied to unmarried mothers and their children. So a pregnant teen often married her baby's father, sometimes with the figurative—if not the literal—image of the girl's father holding a shotgun on the groom to be sure he followed through with the nuptials.

With the sexual revolution of the 1960s, attitudes about such issues loosened up. Although sexual abstinence was still encouraged by many, behavior didn't always follow the ideal—especially among teens. The legalization of abortion also had an effect on what was considered acceptable behavior. Rather than condemning a young unwed mother, some congratulated her for carrying the baby to term, rather than having an abortion.

Teen marriage is generally considered to be a union of adolescents between the ages of thirteen and nineteen. According to eDivorcePapers.com, most teen marriages end in divorce within the first three years. A number of factors contribute to this statistic.

Married teens are at an economic disadvantage. One or both of them will likely need to seek employment. Because of the time involved, one or both may drop out of high school, college, or training programs. With a limited education, they qualify only for low-paying jobs. Someone under eighteen years cannot sign leases or other contracts, so married teens have another disadvantage getting by in the world.

According to Gordon B. Dahl, associate professor and vice chair of the Graduate Studies Department of Economics at the University of California, San Diego, a woman who marries in her teens is 31 percent more likely to live in poverty later in life, and female school dropouts are 11 percent more likely to live in poverty later in life than those who stay in school.

THE TOP TEN BABY NAMES OF 2011

What will you name your baby? According to the U.S. Social Security Administration, these were the top ten names for boys and girls in 2011:

BOYS:	GIRLS:
Jacob	Sophia
Mason	Isabella
William	Emma
Jayden	Olivia
Noah	Ava
Michael	Emily
Ethan	Abigail
Alexander	Madison
Aiden	Mia
Daniel	Chloe

Perhaps even more important are the emotional and psychological issues. Young people often lack coping skills to deal with the kinds of conflicts and obstacles they'll face. Also, many teens have not yet come to terms with who they are. As they grow older, they may develop new interests and experience personality changes. A couple married too young can grow apart simply as a function of maturity.

These stresses can cause couples of any age to divorce. Add them to the stress of new parenthood, and the outlook is negative. However, some teen marriages do last. As with pregnancy, each marriage is different because each person is unique. However, before deciding to marry at a young age, the couple can benefit from marriage counseling either through their place of worship or a counselor in private practice.

CONTINUING EDUCATION

Getting an education or job training is an important way to create a financially stable environment for your child. Fortunately, many public school systems offer alternative programs that let high school students continue their education in a nontraditional way. Or a young mother can earn a high school equivalent diploma by passing the General Educational Development (GED) test. It's also often referred to as a General Education Diploma. The test is developed by the American Council on Education, the coordinating body for America's higher education institutions. Candidates can take online preparation classes, but the test must be taken in person.

♀ BEING A SINGLE MOM

Along with financial help, a young mother needs a support system.

Often, single teen moms face criticism for their choices. Friends, classmates, or even family members may act differently or pass judgment on a teenage mom, leading to isolation. Teen mothers are at greater risk for depression, which can result in bad health outcomes for mom and her baby.

Depending on the situation, this support system can include her immediate and extended family, the father's family, or friends. If you don't know any other teens with babies, you may be able to connect with other new mothers whom you meet in childbirth classes or through your day-care provider.

Support can also include services and programs available in the community. One such program is Women, Infants, and Children (WIC). This government program provides nutrition education, supplemental food, and health care referrals to low-income families even before the baby is born. If you need help breastfeeding, the La Leche League provides services through a network of mothers who can assist you with information and advice.

Many of the issues involved in a teen marriage also apply to young single mothers. Time is something they never have enough of. A baby requires a lot of care. A single mother is likely to have to juggle child care with school or a job—or both. And don't forget sleep. You'll need a lot of it. One tip is to rest while the baby naps, especially at first. Resist the urge to wear yourself out cleaning or doing other physical tasks at naptime. Instead, use the time for light housework, schoolwork, or simple relaxation.

Many universities offer degree programs where students take classes online, rather than in person. Vocational training for such jobs as bookkeeping, paralegal services, and tax preparation, or work in trades like carpentry or plumbing, is also available online or in person. The U.S.

government operates job training and placement programs through the Departments of Labor, Education, and Health and Human Services. Private enterprises also offer programs that help students acquire skills they need in the workplace.

CLASSES FOR COLLEGE CREDIT AND JOB TRAINING ARE AVAILABLE ONLINE, WHICH CAN BE A GOOD WAY FOR A NEW MOTHER TO PREPARE FOR THE WORKFORCE.

Even if you must support yourself financially, time constraints may prevent full-time employment, especially if you're still in school. Part-time jobs often pay less per hour than full-time ones, but every bit helps. Look for a job with an understanding boss and flexible hours or one that can be done from home. Some job sites offer child care to employees, so consider applying for employment at one of them.

You may have other financial resources to draw upon. Your family may contribute to expenses. Or the baby's father or his family may be able to help. (Keep in mind that if the baby's father is identified on the birth certificate, he is legally required to help.)

CHAPTER 2

PREPARATION FOR CHILDBIRTH

Today's mothers have many choices for labor and birth. These range from medication-free home births to total medical intervention. You might even choose to have your baby underwater.

CHILDBIRTH EDUCATION

It's perfectly normal to have some fears about childbirth. Childbirth education helps new mothers know what to expect. Childbirth classes will arm you with information, reassurance, and coping techniques to ease your mind before labor and help you through it when it starts. In some states, Medicaid pays for childbirth education for low-income mothers. Or you may qualify for a reduced fee.

You can choose the type of classes you want. You have many choices, and many of the methods share the same attitudes toward birth as a normal process. Among the

most popular methods today are hospital-based classes, Lamaze, the Bradley Method, Birthing from Within, and birth hypnosis. Hospital-based classes often offer instruction in the stages of labor, pain management, potential complications, and medical procedures. Your practitioner can

CHILDBIRTH EDUCATION CLASSES OFTEN INCLUDE INFORMATION ABOUT BABY CARE, AS WELL AS LABOR AND DELIVERY. THE BABY'S FATHER OR ANOTHER COACH CAN TAKE THE CLASSES ALONGSIDE THE PREGNANT WOMAN.

recommend classes, or you can look for them in the community.

Lamaze classes show pregnant women how to use breathing and other strategies to help them get through labor and birth. Its philosophy includes a holistic view of natural, normal childbirth. It encourages waiting for labor to start on its own and letting women eat, drink, and move around during labor. And it empowers women to make informed decisions should medical intervention be desired or necessary.

The Bradley Method focuses on the benefits of drug-free birth, for both the mother and baby. It uses slow, deep breathing and other techniques to help the mother achieve complete relaxation. Classes also include information about nutrition, exercise, bonding, and breastfeeding. The method stresses the importance of a birthing coach, who is close to the mother and who is likely to be active in the baby's life.

Birthing from Within is a method that uses information along with spiritual and creative art projects to help mothers-to-be deal with expectations, fears, and other emotions concerning childbirth. Instructors don't promote any particular childbirth method, but they support natural birth if that is what the mother wants.

Several types of birth hypnosis teach women to train themselves to deal with pain without fear or anxiety. Some new mothers give the method rave reviews. Others report it didn't help them at all.

CESAREAN SECTIONS

Most women give birth vaginally, but some have a surgical procedure called a cesarean section, or C-section. Under a local or general anesthetic, a doctor cuts into the mother's abdomen and lifts the baby out. The surgery has been used since ancient times, but most cesarean procedures back then were performed to save the baby from mothers who had already died in the birthing process or were dying and could not be helped.

A C-section is major surgery. Many are performed for medical reasons involving the mother or baby's health, and a few are requested by the mother. According to Listening to Mothers II, a national survey of more than 1,500 mothers who gave birth in 2005, less than 1 percent of mothers who had a first-time C-section had requested it. In nearly 90 percent of the cases, a physician made the decision either before or during labor.

However, a 2010 poll of more than five thousand members of the American Congress of Obstetricians and Gynecologists reported in the journal *Obstetrics and Gynecology* found that 29 percent said they performed more C-sections today than in the past because they feared lawsuits should something go wrong with a vaginal birth. Like all surgeries, C-sections carry risks. According to Time.com, the surgery increases the odds of such complications as bleeding or blood clots. They should not be taken lightly.

DEVELOPING A BIRTH PLAN

After you've investigated ways to deal with labor and birth, as well as whether you'd like to have your baby in a hospital, a birth center, or your home, it's a good idea to develop a birth plan. A birth plan is a list of your preferences for what happens during and after labor and birth.

Developing a birth plan can help pregnant mothers communicate their wishes about labor and birth to the practitioner who will attend the birth.

A birth plan includes such items as:

- Where will the baby be born?

- Who will assist the process?

- How do you want to handle pain relief?

- What kind of environment do you want for childbirth?

- What back-up plan is in place should you change your mind about pain management or if an emergency arises?

- What choices of positions will you want during labor and delivery?

- Do you want soft music playing and/or the lights dimmed for the baby's birth?

- Which newborn tests can be done right away, and which can be delayed or declined?

- Do you want to hold and feed the baby right away?

Discuss your plan with the practitioner who will attend the birth. Remember, these are your preferences. Actual

events may differ. Having a birth plan in place doesn't guarantee you'll get everything on your list. Unexpected occurrences may dictate different choices. Or you might change your mind during the process. However, a birth

YOGA BENEFITS INCLUDE IMPROVED CIRCULATION, STRENGTH, FLEXIBILITY, AND BLOOD PRESSURE, AS WELL AS RELAXATION TECHNIQUES FOR PREGNANCY, LABOR, BIRTH, AND THE TIME AFTER BIRTH.

plan allows your childbirth team to work with you while considering your health and that of the baby. A birth plan can also help you choose a health care provider and the place you want to have your baby.

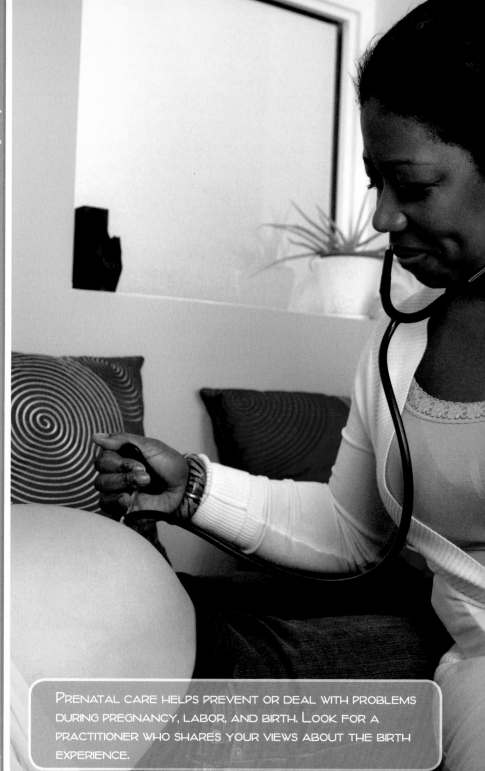

Prenatal care helps prevent or deal with problems during pregnancy, labor, and birth. Look for a practitioner who shares your views about the birth experience.

Choosing a Practitioner

You can get labor and delivery care from an obstetrician or a family practice doctor. Doctors may practice in private offices or clinics. You might also get prenatal care from a certified nurse-midwife, who practices at a hospital or birth center, or a certified professional midwife, who practices at a birth center and at the client's home for home births. All midwives have a connection with a medical doctor they can call on if a problem or emergency occurs. To find a practitioner, ask for referrals from your primary care doctor or friends and family.

TERMINAL MECONIUM

Meconium is the substance that comprises an infant's first several bowel movements. Most babies have their first bowel movement after birth. Occasionally, the fetus will pass the meconium while still in the bag of waters.

Some have the movement during birth itself. Childbirth practitioners call this terminal meconium. They may want to immediately suction the baby's mouth and breathing passages to prevent lung problems. They may say something like, "We have terminal meconium." Then they whisk the baby away from the mother and rush to work on the baby.

Witnessing such activity has made more than one new mother worry that her baby has died. Rest assured, most babies in this situation are perfectly healthy or have only mild, temporary lung issues. In some cases, though, especially if the meconium was released into the amniotic fluid, the problems can be severe.

Also consider using the services of a doula to advocate for you during labor and birth. A doula is a nonmedical person who provides physical and emotional support during pregnancy, labor, birth, and the period after the baby arrives. Doulas often work in conjunction with midwives. The doula's services include such techniques as massage, aromatherapy, visualization, and positioning during labor. The doula also acts as a spokesperson for the mother when communicating preferences to the medical staff. Depending on the arrangement with the new mother, the doula may also visit her and the child at home after the birth or help answer questions about breastfeeding or other baby care.

Your choice will depend on a number of factors. What kind of birth plan do you want to create? You may choose a traditional hospital setting. Or you may prefer an alternative birth center or have your baby at home to avoid medical interventions like fetal monitoring, pain medicine or other drugs, or C-sections that may not be necessary if you and the baby are at low risk for complications.

When deciding on a provider, ask about the professional's philosophy concerning labor and birth. Discuss your choices of hospital, birth center, or home. Other factors include the office location and hours, and whether you'll see the same person for all prenatal appointments. Also think about the person's personality and whether you feel comfortable with him or her.

You'll also want to line up a birth coach—someone to coach you through labor. If the baby's father is in your life, it could be him. It could also be someone you trust or someone who emotionally supports you, such as a family member. This person should attend your childbirth education classes with you to learn what his or her role will be. You and the coach should practice techniques before you go into labor. Sometime during the pregnancy, look for a pediatrician or family practice doctor to provide health care for the baby after he or she is born.

Your doctor, family, or friends can recommend candidates. Interview several to be sure they support your preferences about feeding, vaccines, infant sleep, and other issues.

Myths and Facts

Myth

You can't get pregnant while you're breastfeeding.

Fact

While breastfeeding tends to postpone ovulation, ovulation can still occur. Talk to your doctor about what type of birth control works best for nursing moms.

Myth

If the mother's water breaks, it means she is in labor.

Fact

Most women do go into labor within twenty-four hours of the release of amniotic fluid, but the start of contractions is a more reliable measure. Some women's water doesn't break until they're well into labor. In rare instances, the baby is born with the amniotic sac intact. This is known as "being born in the caul," which is associated with myths and legends worldwide.

Myth

The umbilical cord that connects the baby to the mother should be cut as soon as the baby is delivered.

Fact

When a baby is born, blood continues to pulse through the umbilical cord. It's best to wait until the pulsing stops to give the infant a chance to get the last bit of life support from the placenta. This additional blood can help prevent anemia during the baby's first several months.

UNPLANNED
SAFE SEX
BIRTH PLAN
Pregnancy
PARENTHOOD
MOTHERHOOD
single mom
TEEN
Childbirth
CONCEPTION
CHAPTER 3

Your Pregnancy

If you decide to carry the baby to term, one of your first steps should be to seek prenatal health care. To help stay healthy during the pregnancy, you'll need regular check-ups. Your health care provider may order screening tests for you or your baby. Prenatal care is especially important for teens. It gives you the opportunity to get information about nutrition, exercise, labor, and the birthing process. Teens often have low birth-weight babies, who have a higher risk of serious illness. Also, teens commonly have poor diets without many of the nutrients that growing babies need.

Your baby eats what you eat and drinks what you drink. Eating a wide variety of foods and taking a daily prenatal vitamin will help ensure that you and the baby get the nutrients you need. Weight gain is extremely important during this time, and not gaining an appropriate amount of weight can result in low birth weight and lead to developmental problems for the baby. Throughout the pregnancy, follow a healthy diet that is low in sugar and high in protein, vitamins, and minerals. Especially important are iron, calcium, protein, folic acid, and vitamins A, B_6, B_{12}, and C in the right amounts.

According to Brenda J. Lane and Ilana T. Kirsch, authors of the *Knack Pregnancy Guide*, you'll need 3,300 international units (IUs) of vitamin A each day. But too much of the vitamin can harm the growing baby. Be aware that some acne treatments have high levels of this vitamin. Consult your health care provider before taking these or any other medicines while pregnant. Also avoid alcohol, nicotine, and recreational drugs. These can have devastating effects on the baby before or after he or she is born (if you are breastfeeding).

Staying hydrated while you're expecting is also important. Recommended drinks include water, skim milk, green tea, and cranberry juice (not cranberry cocktail or juice drinks) diluted with water or seltzer.

For a healthy pregnancy, you also need physical activity. Along with being good for the baby, exercise reduces some of the discomforts that pregnant women often experience. It reduces the risk of preterm labor, increases stamina for the labor and birth, and contributes to recovery afterward. Always check with your health care provider before embarking on an exercise plan.

Some activities should be avoided, especially horseback riding, downhill skiing, scuba diving, gymnastics, and contact sports like basketball. After the first three months, avoid exercises where you lie on your back. Some

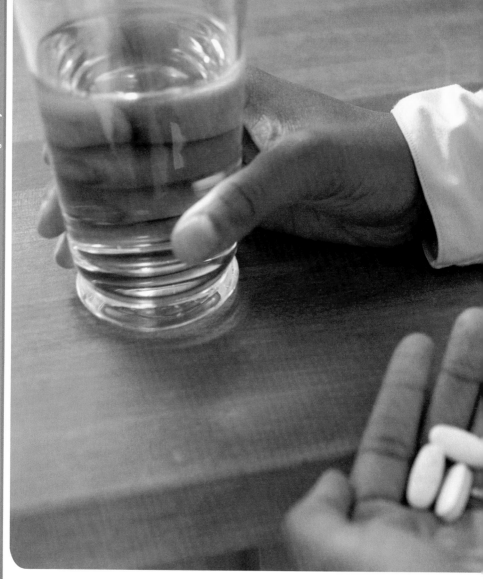

good choices—especially in early pregnancy—are low-impact exercises like walking, swimming, and water aerobics (but avoid hot tubs). Or join a prenatal exercise class led by a reputable organization.

YOUR GROWING BABY

One of the first items on your prenatal agenda should be figuring out the baby's due date. To estimate the date, use

> A BALANCED DIET ALONG WITH VITAMIN AND MINERAL SUPPLEMENTS DESIGNED FOR PREGNANT WOMEN CAN HELP ENSURE THAT BOTH THE MOTHER AND GROWING BABY GET THE PROPER NUTRIENTS.

the first day of your most recent period as the starting point. Then count forty weeks ahead. It is only an educated guess based on average human gestation, the time a baby grows in the uterus. If you're unsure of when your last period began, or if your last period was unusually light, you may need an ultrasound between the eighth week and eighteenth week of pregnancy to determine when to expect birth.

First Trimester (Weeks 1 to 12)

The forty weeks of pregnancy are grouped into three stages of three months, and each stage is called a trimester. Each trimester is characterized by different signs and developments in the mother and child. The first twelve weeks mark hormonal changes in the mother. These changes affect most organ systems. In addition to early symptoms of pregnancy, you may experience food cravings or a distaste for certain foods, constipation, headache, heartburn, and weight gain. In early pregnancy, you might even lose weight. You may experience all of these symptoms or some or none of them.

During the first trimester, the baby, called an embryo, is busy forming the heart, brain, and spinal cord. Little stumps that will become arms and legs appear. The baby is approximately 0.04 inches (0.1 centimeters) "tall." At eight weeks, the baby has a regular heartbeat. Major body structures and organs—including sex organs—have begun to form. Arms and legs lengthen, and fingers and toes start to develop. The eyes, which now have eyelids, move from the side to the front of the face. The baby is about 1 inch (2.5 cm) long and weighs 0.12 ounces (3 grams). From the end of eight weeks to birth, the baby is called a fetus.

Over the next four weeks, the fetus will grow to about 3 inches (8 cm) long and weigh close to 1 ounce (28 g). Nerves and muscles work together well enough for the fetus to make a fist. External sex organs have formed. The eyelids close and will not open until the end of the second trimester. This protects developing eyes.

At seven weeks a human embryo is already developing upper limbs, fingers, and a face. Although the eyes have formed, they can't yet function. Brain development at this time is rapid.

Second Trimester (Weeks 13 to 28)

By the thirteenth week of pregnancy, tiredness and nausea ease. The abdomen expands to make room for the growing fetus. You may experience aches and pains in your back, abdomen, groin, or thighs. Skin around the nipples may darken. You might notice stretch marks on the abdomen, breast, thighs, or buttocks, or see a line on the skin between the pubic hairline and navel.

Your hands may feel numb or tingle. In some women, hormonal changes cause fluid retention and increase the risk of carpal tunnel syndrome. Symptoms usually disappear after childbirth. You may also experience itching on the abdomen, hands, or feet, or swelling of the face, fingers, or ankles. Call your health care provider if the itching is accompanied by fatigue, nausea, loss of appetite, or yellowish skin or eyes. This can indicate liver trouble. Also call your provider if you have sudden or excessive swelling or gain weight too fast. These symptoms can indicate a complication of the pregnancy.

At sixteen weeks, the fetus is getting a more complete skeleton as bone continues to grow. Skin begins to form. The fetus exhibits the sucking reflex. He or she is 4 to 5 inches (10 to 13 cm) long and weighs about 3 ounces (85 g). By twenty weeks—halfway through the gestation period—you might feel a slight fluttering that some describe as butterflies. At first, the sensation is so slight that you may doubt whether you actually felt something. As the baby grows and becomes more active, you'll feel more

♀ RECOMMENDED FOODS FOR PREGNANT WOMEN

Foods high in the nutrients that pregnant women and growing fetuses need include a wide variety of great choices. Nutrients that are especially important are iron, calcium, protein, folic acid, and vitamins A, B_6, B_{12}, and C. Be sure to take a daily prenatal vitamin and choose foods loaded with what you need.

Iron
Bran flakes
Fortified cereal
Turkey

Calcium
Cheese
Milk
Yogurt

Protein
Almonds
Beef
Chicken
Eggs
Turkey

Vitamin A
Romaine lettuce
Spinach
Tomatoes

Vitamin B_6
Bananas
Chicken
Salmon

Vitamin B_{12}
Beef
Salmon

Vitamin C
Raspberries
Tomatoes
Romaine lettuce

Folic Acid
Asparagus
Bran flakes
Enriched breads and cereals
Lentils
Red beans
Strawberries

movement. At this point, the baby can hear and swallow. He or she has eyebrows, eyelashes, fingernails, and toe-nails. The length is about 6 inches (15 cm), and the weight has increased to about 9 ounces (255 g).

Between twenty-four and twenty-eight weeks, the baby is fine-tuning. Taste buds, footprints, and fingerprints form. Hair grows on the head. Sex organs are developed and in place. The baby regularly sleeps and wakes. He or she has grown to about 12 inches (30 cm) long and weighs about 1.5 pounds (0.68 kilograms).

THIRD TRIMESTER (WEEKS 29 TO 40)

The growing baby presses against the mother's organs. You may experience some of the same signs of the second trimester along with shortness of breath, heartburn, leaky breasts, or hemorrhoids. You may have trouble sleeping or notice contractions that may or may not lead to labor. Contractions are the periodic tightening and relaxing of the uterus.

During this time, the cervix thins and softens, which helps open the birth canal. You'll feel forceful kicks or punches that leave no doubt that you felt something. You may even see the baby's heel pushing against your abdomen.

By the thirty-second week, the fetus has a complete but soft skeleton. The eyes open and close. The lungs are still developing. The baby gains weight faster than before— about 0.5 pounds (0.22 kg) per week. At thirty-six weeks, the baby weighs about 6 pounds (3 kg) and "stands" 16

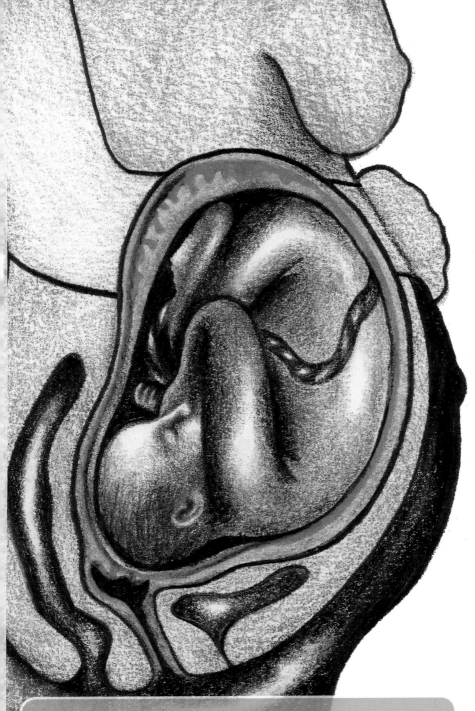

By thirty-seven weeks the fetus is considered full term. He or she can survive outside the mother's womb. Most babies are in a head-down position for birth.

to 19 inches (41 to 48 cm). At 37 weeks, the baby is considered full term. The organs can function on their own. The baby can survive outside the mother's body. You're in the home stretch!

COMMON PREGNANCY COMPLICATIONS

Health problems for the mother or baby during pregnancy are known as complications. If you already had health problems before you were pregnant, they can continue to affect you during your pregnancy. So can medicines you're taking to treat them. Some common pre-pregnancy issues include asthma, depression, diabetes, eating disorders, epilepsy, high blood pressure, migraines, obesity, sexually transmitted infections, thyroid disease, and noncancerous tumors in the uterus. Be sure your prenatal care provider knows every medicine you take. He or she may want you to replace or discontinue the drugs or use a different treatment.

Some complications in mothers-to-be arise during pregnancy. Many disappear after delivery. Fortunately, most of them can be managed during pregnancy with proper health care. These may include such conditions as:

- Anemia, a low number of red blood cells that causes weakness, fatigue, pale skin, or shortness of breath

- Depression, feelings of extreme sadness during or after pregnancy

- Ectopic pregnancy, a fertilized egg that implants outside the uterus, typically in the fallopian tubes, which connect the ovaries to the uterus

- Gestational diabetes, or high blood sugar

- Severe and persistent nausea or vomiting

- Preeclampsia (also known as toxemia), a condition marked by high blood pressure, swelling of hands and face, stomach pain, and headaches

Fetal problems, such as poor growth or heart trouble, are also considered complications

UNPLANNED

SAFE SEX

BIRTH PLAN

Pregnancy

PARENTHOOD

MOTHERHOOD

single mom

TEEN

Childbirth

CONCEPTION

CHAPTER 4

GETTING EQUIPPED FOR MOTHERHOOD AND BABY CARE

By the second trimester (or even before), your clothes are likely to feel tight around the waist. Maternity clothes are designed for comfort for the mother-to-be. They often have drawstring or elastic waists, or come with stretchy panels that give as your abdomen grows.

When shopping for other items, keep in mind the seasons you'll wear them. A sleeveless blouse won't do you much good in the dead of winter. Neither will a bulky sweater in summer. Most pregnant teens have little money for maternity clothes. If you're one of them, consider shopping at thrift stores for prices lower than retail. You might be able to borrow clothes from a relative or friend. Even if you have a nice budget, remember that you'll need maternity clothes only for six or seven months, so resist the urge to fill your closet. Also, your size may change over the nine

SOME MATERNITY PANTS HAVE A STRETCHY PANEL IN THE FRONT TO ACCOMMODATE THE MOTHER'S GROWING UTERUS. AVOID THE URGE TO BUY TOO MANY CLOTHES YOU WON'T NEED FOR LONG.

months, so plan to shop again several times as the pregnancy progresses.

WHAT BABIES NEED

Stores that cater to new parents have plenty of items in stock. However, you won't need one of each. You won't need many of the available baby goods at all. A newborn's needs are simple. He or she needs to eat, stay dry and warm, and have a place to sleep. Shop for things you would need if the baby arrived today.

If you plan to nurse your baby, you won't need bottle systems. However, if you plan to return to school or work and someone will be baby-sitting, look into buying a breast pump that lets you express and store breast milk in bottles that the caregiver can use. Even if you plan to bottle-feed, you won't need a case of bottles. Get just a few to get started. You can get more later. Or you might want to change the type of bottle you use.

Keeping baby dry is easily solved with a supply of cloth or disposable diapers. These come in different

BABIES' NEEDS ARE SIMPLE. YOU DON'T NEED EVERY GADGET IN THE BABY SECTION! REMEMBER THAT BABIES GROW FAST. THEY WILL OUTGROW NEWBORN CLOTHES VERY SOON.

sizes to fit preemies up through about two years of age. You'll want to start with newborn size. Buy only a package or two until you see how big the baby is. Remember, babies grow fast. You don't want a huge supply of diapers that are too small to use. You'll also need a diaper pail for dirty diapers, a diaper bag for quick trips, and some burp cloths to use when feeding the infant.

♀ THE 5-1-1 PLAN

Contractions may or may not indicate the beginning of the childbirth process. Some contractions occur but fail to continue at regular intervals. They may stop altogether. To avoid unnecessary trips to the hospital or birth center, follow the 5-1-1 plan.

Use a stopwatch or wristwatch with a second hand to keep track of when each contraction starts and ends. That is the duration of the contraction. Also monitor the time from the

WHEN CONTRACTIONS FIRST BEGIN, THEY MAY OR MAY NOT SIGNAL THE START OF LABOR. TIME BOTH HOW LONG THEY LAST AND HOW FAR APART THEY ARE.

start of one contraction to the start of the next one. That is the frequency. When the contraction frequency is every FIVE minutes and the duration is ONE minute each, and that frequency and duration have been maintained for ONE hour, it's time to call the doctor or midwife.

Caution: Call your practitioner (or head for the hospital or birth center) if:

- You start with contractions that last one minute and come less than five minutes apart.
- Your water breaks and the fluid is green or dark yellow.
- You are bleeding heavily or experiencing severe pain.
- You're worried or afraid.

Keeping baby warm means clothes and blankets. Depending on the season, look for T-shirts or "onesies," short-sleeved or long-sleeved bodysuits with bottom snaps that easily tuck into pants or shorts. One-piece sleepers or sleep sacks are great, especially for the first several weeks. Sleep sacks are similar to sleeping bags used for camping, except the top part has sleeves. It's like a blanket with a built-in sleeper.

Newborns often need hats and socks to keep warm. (To wash baby socks, put them in a mesh bag together before throwing them in a washing machine. They'll be easier to match when they come out.) You'll also need some soft, lightweight blankets called receiving blankets.

In its five-year policy update in 2011, the American Academy of Pediatrics stated that bumper pads pose a suffocation or strangulation risk and should not be used in cribs.

If you know your baby's gender, get a few cute outfits for visitors or visiting. Don't waste money on clothes the infant may never wear (or will quickly grow out of).

WHERE WILL THE BABY SLEEP?

A place for the baby to sleep depends in part on your parenting philosophy. When the baby is first born, he or she will need to feed every couple of hours. You might want to put the baby to sleep in a crib in a separate room. Or, for ease in getting to the baby in the middle of the night, consider a bassinet or cradle in your room. Or use a portable crib that you can also use when visiting or traveling.

Some mothers choose to bring their babies to bed with them. Co-sleeping makes breastfeeding easier during the night. It also contributes to the mother-child bond and helps the infant sleep better. But there are some risks. A baby should never sleep with the mother on a sofa, waterbed, or very soft mattress. Other dangers include mothers who are overtired or have used any alcohol or medications that make them sleepy.

Precautions also include using a firm mattress, covering the baby with a small blanket instead of adult bedding, keeping the baby away from pillows, and ensuring the baby cannot fall between the mattress and the wall or headboard. You should also use a guardrail on the baby's side of the adult bed or a "sidecar" baby bed that attaches to the adult bed. Be sure that the fabric liner is securely attached or not used at all to prevent the infant from

A humidifier helps ease congestion in infants. It also works for older children and adults. You'll need one sooner or later, so buy it before you need it.

becoming trapped between the edge of the mattress and the side of the sleeper.

Equipping the Nursery

Make a list of what you'll need after the baby is born. A new mom needs a sling or soft infant carrier to keep the baby close during the day. You'll want a swing, bouncy seat, or other item where you can put the baby when you can't carry him or her.

Sooner or later, every baby will need a humidifier. Humidifiers release water particles into the air, increasing the humidity of a room. This can help ease congestion, especially important for infants, who should not be given any cold medication. Get one before you need it so that you won't have to drag a sick child to the store to buy one when you need it. And before you know it, you'll want a stroller and a highchair. An audio and/or video baby monitor will help you check on a sleeping baby (or older playing child) from another room in the house. Whether you're nursing or bottle-feeding, look for a nursing pillow. It supports the infant while you're holding or feeding him or her.

Check for Crib Safety

Keep an eye out for used or borrowed gear. If you're lucky, friends and family may buy some of the items for you as gifts. Today's new mothers have lots of choices in selecting baby furniture. Many cribs can later be converted into toddler beds with side rails and twin or full-size.

The U.S. Consumer Product Safety Commission (CPSC) has issued guidelines for safe crib use. New furniture sold online or in stores is required to conform to these rules. However, beware of older cribs. Avoid drop-side cribs. Check current safety standards from the (CPSC). Decline offers or purchases of cribs that don't meet them. As of 2011, the rules included:

- The crib should have a firm mattress with no space between the mattress and the frame.
- Screws, brackets, and other hardware must be in place and properly installed with none missing, loose, or broken.
- The maximum space between crib slats is 2⅜ inches (6 cm). This space prevents a baby's body from falling through them. No slats should be missing or broken.
- Any corner posts must be no higher than 1⁄16 inches (1.6 millimeters) to prevent the child's clothing from catching on them.
- There should be no cutouts (holes) in the head-board or footboard where a baby's head could get trapped.

For mesh-sided cribs or playpens, the mesh should be smaller than ¼ inch (6.35 mm) in diameter. The mesh should have no tears, holes, or loose threads, and it should be securely attached to the top rail and floor of the item. The top rail should have no tears or holes. No staples should be loose, missing, or exposed.

ON THE GO

Perhaps the most important piece of equipment that babies need is a properly installed car seat. Most hospitals will ask to see your car seat before letting you take the baby home. If you borrow or buy a used car seat, be sure it has not been involved in a car accident, even a minor "fender bender." Also check with the manufacturer or online to be sure that the model has not been involved in a safety recall.

Choose a car seat based on the child's age, height, and weight. Some are made only for infants. Others convert as the child grows. According to the National Highway Traffic Safety Administration (NHTSA), your child should stay in the same size seat as long as he or she fits the height and weight requirements. All children younger than thirteen years should ride in the back seat.

Carefully follow your vehicle's owner's manual and the car seat manufacturer's installation instructions. Certified technicians are available to check your installation for free. Check the NHTSA's Web site to find an inspection station near you.

Ten Great Questions
TO ASK A HEALTH CARE PROVIDER

1.
Do antibiotics or other medications affect the reliability of oral birth control pills?

2.
Can pregnancy result from having sex during my period?

3.
What does pregnancy have to do with bladder control?

4.
What kind of childbirth preparation do you recommend?

5.
How much and what kind of exercise should I do during pregnancy?

6.
What if I need to take medicine during pregnancy?

7.
How much weight can I safely gain while I'm pregnant?

8.
What are the risks of C-section compared with vaginal birth?

9.
How can I reduce the risk of sudden infant death syndrome?

10.
Which tests and medicines do my baby need at birth?

CHAPTER 5

HAVING YOUR BABY

Near the end of your pregnancy, you may feel a burst of energy. You might feel like cleaning the entire house or doing endless loads of laundry. This is called a nesting urge. Labor is likely to start within the next day or two. If you feel like mowing all the lawns in the neighborhood, conserve your energy instead. You'll need it soon.

Labor is the birth process. It begins with contractions of the uterus. Some describe them as cramping similar to the pulling and tightening sensation in the calf known as a "charley horse." Others describe the feeling as pressure in the back or abdomen. The contractions get harder and closer together as birth nears. They cause the top part of the uterus to tighten and thicken while the bottom part stretches and relaxes. This helps the fetus move into the birth canal and out into the world.

Labor has four stages. For about 75 percent of first-time mothers, it lasts between fourteen and twenty-four hours, according to Tori Kropp, R.N., author of *The Joy of Pregnancy*.

STAGE ONE

The first stage of labor takes the longest. It is also the easiest to manage. There are three phases to this stage:

- Early phase
- Active phase
- Transition phase

The early phase lasts about eight to twelve hours, and most laboring women stay home during this time. This phase thins the lower third of the uterus (called the cervix) and begins to widen it. Contractions are irregular both in frequency and intensity. Try not to focus too much on these early contractions. They are warming up the body for the harder and more frequent contractions to come.

You may feel aches in the back, legs, or lower abdomen. There may be diarrhea or a mucous or bloody vaginal discharge.

This is called "bloody show," and it's usually a reddish brown color. (If the discharge is bright red, call your practitioner.)

If this phase begins at night, try to stay asleep. Even a short nap can be beneficial. You can also read or watch television. During the day, stay upright or take a walk. (But it's not the time for a 5K run.) Stay active, but don't wear yourself out.

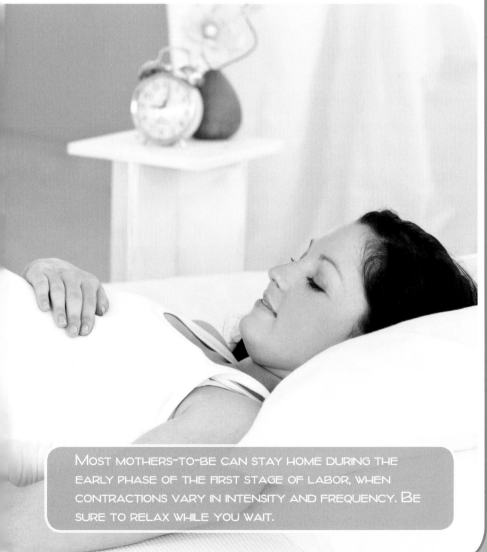

MOST MOTHERS-TO-BE CAN STAY HOME DURING THE EARLY PHASE OF THE FIRST STAGE OF LABOR, WHEN CONTRACTIONS VARY IN INTENSITY AND FREQUENCY. BE SURE TO RELAX WHILE YOU WAIT.

ACTIVE AND TRANSITION PHASES

The active phase typically lasts from four to six hours. The cervix continues to widen, but it's not yet time for the baby to pass through it. While you might have been joking around during the first phase, one sign that you're in the active phase is a total loss of your sense of humor.

Contractions are on a regular schedule about two or three minutes apart. They last about a minute and are intense enough to keep you from talking or moving. This is a time to use breathing and relaxation techniques. Between contractions, you will get a little rest and be able to regroup or reposition yourself.

The transition phase of early labor lasts only about one to three hours. This is the time the cervix widens to its maximum diameter of between 2.8 and 3.9 inches (7 and 10 cm). This phase moves the action from stage one to stage two. Contractions last longer (about ninety seconds) and come one or two minutes apart; these are the hardest to deal with. The transition phase is also when some women who first chose natural childbirth think they can't take any more intense or frequent contractions and ask for pain relief medication. For most women, however, stage two offers some relief from the transition phase.

STAGE TWO

During the second stage, you'll actively participate in helping your baby move through the birth canal. This is the pushing stage and is similar to but more intense than having a bowel movement.

If you have not had pain medication, your body will tell you when to push. The urge occurs with each contraction. You will bear down until the contraction ends. If you are medicated, your birth team will tell you when to push. The time between contractions often increases during this stage, which gives you more time to rest between them. Stage two lasts about one to three hours (depending somewhat on the size of the fetus). It ends with the baby's birth.

It's Not Over?

Soon after the baby's birth, the placenta detaches and the uterus expels it. The placenta, also called the after-birth, forms inside the uterus from the same cells that create the embryo. It supplies nutrients and oxygen from the mother's blood. It also transfers waste products from the baby's blood to the mother's, where the mother's kidneys process it. The placenta helps start labor by producing necessary hormones.

Within about five to thirty minutes after the baby's birth, you'll again push. This time, the process will be much easier than when you pushed out the baby. Once the placenta is delivered, the practitioner will press on your abdomen or massage it until the uterus firms. A firm uterus prevents excessive bleeding from the detachment of the placenta.

The two hours after you give birth comprise stage four. This is known as the immediate postpartum period. If you plan to breastfeed, it starts now. It's also OK to eat or drink what you like or just rest. During this time, your caregivers will observe you to see that the uterus is contracting. They'll also check for excessive bleeding.

The mother-baby bonding process starts as soon as the baby is born. Many new mothers hold the baby skin-to-skin during the first minutes after birth.

NEWBORN HEALTH CARE

An Apgar test measures five signs of a newborn's health. It helps medical personnel decide if the baby needs extra medical care. It tests the baby's heart rate, breathing, muscle tone, reflexes, and skin color. Health care providers perform the test twice. The first time is one minute after birth. The second time is four minutes later, when the baby is five minutes old. Apgar scores range from zero to ten. A score of seven or higher indicates a healthy baby. A baby who scores lower than that on the second screening needs additional medical attention and close monitoring.

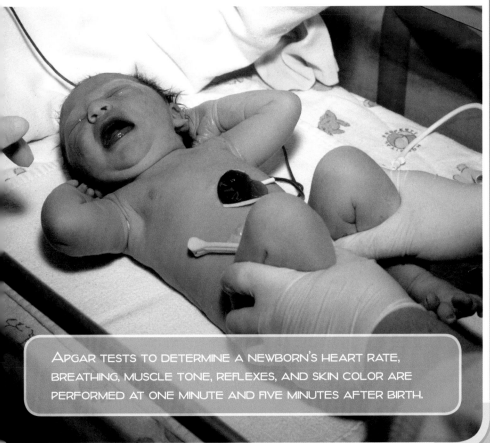

APGAR TESTS TO DETERMINE A NEWBORN'S HEART RATE, BREATHING, MUSCLE TONE, REFLEXES, AND SKIN COLOR ARE PERFORMED AT ONE MINUTE AND FIVE MINUTES AFTER BIRTH.

Newborns need some additional tests, medicine, and procedures—some required by law. Eye drops are often applied to prevent blindness that can result from sexually transmitted infections, like gonorrhea or chlamydia. Some parents at low risk for STIs choose not to have these drops administered to their new baby.

Newborns usually have low levels of vitamin K, a vitamin necessary for blood clotting. The American Academy of Pediatrics (AAP) recommends a shot of vitamin K to prevent excessive bleeding. Another test is a metabolic screening. A small blood sample is taken from the baby's heel to test for phenylketonuria (PKU), hypothyroidism, galactosemia, and sickle cell disease. If the baby has any of these diseases, early treatment can prevent developmental disabilities, organ damage, blindness, or even death.

Newborns also get a hearing test. If a hearing disability is found early, the child can get a head start with treatment that can prevent speech and language delays. Finally, a vaccine that protects against the hepatitis B virus (HPV) is recommended for newborns. The vaccine can prevent a lifelong infection, as well as liver damage and death. Full protection requires three shots during the first eighteen months of age. The AAP and CDC recommend the first shot before leaving the hospital.

Medical personnel also check the baby's temperature, breathing, and heart rate, and they measure the baby's weight, length, and head circumference. They'll also bathe the baby and clean the area around the severed umbilical cord.

EARLY ARRIVALS

Some babies are born early. They're premature and are often referred to as "preemies." By definition, a premature birth is one that occurs before the thirty-seventh week of pregnancy. According to PreemieSurvival.org, about 12 percent of all pregnancies in the United States are premature.

Premature birth is among the leading causes of American infant death. But thanks to today's technology, many preemies survive. The longer the fetus developed in the uterus, the better the chance of survival. Again, according to PreemieSurvival .org, babies born at twenty-three weeks have a 17 percent survival rate. Just one more week improves the rate to 39 percent. Half of babies born at twenty-five weeks survive. By thirty-two weeks, most preemies survive.

In the past, babies were whisked away from their mothers in order for these interventions to be performed. However, many new mothers understand the need to bond with the baby as soon as possible after birth. The additional medical activities can be conducted an hour or so after birth. If you want to hold or nurse your baby right away, discuss the issue with your doctor or midwife during prenatal visits.

INDUCING LABOR

In some circumstances, practitioners may induce labor to get the birth process going. One reason to consider induced labor is a pregnancy that goes beyond forty-two weeks, when a woman is considered post-term. Some medical reasons to induce labor include:

- The fetus is growing so large, vaginal delivery may become impossible if labor continues.
- The fetus is growing too slowly and doctors think the baby will be safer outside the uterus.
- The mother's health is threatened, or a medical condition is getting worse.
- The amniotic fluid level is too low.

Some women request induction for convenience or other personal reasons. In the United States, elective induction of labor is one of the most commonly performed medical procedures. According to Kropp, 30 percent of all cases of induced labor in America are for the mother's convenience.

But choosing to induce labor is not without risk and therefore should be considered carefully. According to the Mayo Clinic, induced labor often results in a C-section, especially in women who have never given birth before. Labor is a natural process that most often needs no medical intervention to begin. In most cases, it's best to let the baby arrive when he or she is ready.

PARENTHOOD
MOTHERHOOD
single mom
UNPLANNED
SAFE SEX
BIRTH PLAN
TEEN
Childbirth
CONCEPTION
Pregnancy

CHAPTER 6

WHY BABIES CRY

Newborns are helpless. They cannot feed themselves. They cannot move to where food is. They can't keep themselves safe. Or warm. Or dry. They have no language to communicate their needs. So what do they do? They cry.

Crying is normal. In fact, it is a survival tool. It's the only way that babies can get the care they need.

A newborn's cry signals his or her entry into the world. Most babies cry the moment they breathe air for the first time. As they grow, they cry for different reasons. Through trial and error, mothers discover why babies cry in different situations. That helps them meet the child's needs.

What's important is to respond to any baby's cry quickly. Letting him or her "cry it out" can contribute to feelings of insecurity. Sometimes a baby just needs to feel close contact with the mother or another person. Sometimes clothing is too tight or too scratchy. Or the crying may result from a number of other reasons. Stay calm and try to figure out what's wrong and what to do about it.

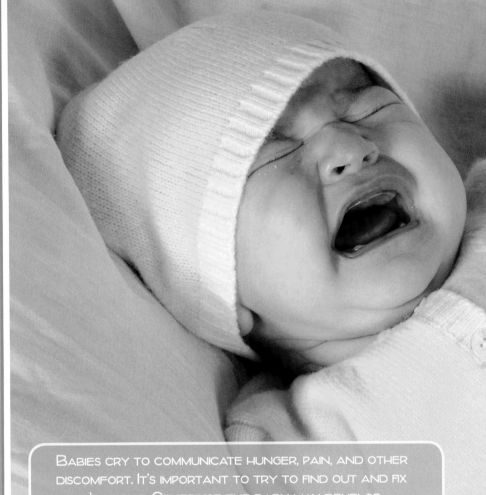

Babies cry to communicate hunger, pain, and other discomfort. It's important to try to find out and fix what's wrong. Otherwise the baby may develop insecurities.

Feed Me

Hunger is a big reason why babies cry. For the first month, most infants need nourishment about eight to twelve times a day. Their little stomachs can't hold enough milk to supply the calories they need less often than that. At the very least, a newborn needs to be fed about every four hours. So hunger is your first best guess as to why your baby is crying.

Babies who are breast-fed may be sensitive to food or drink consumed by their mothers and transferred to breast milk. Caffeine and spicy food can cause occasional irritability or stomachaches. If you think this is the case, reduce your caffeine intake or avoid foods that may be at fault.

If your baby cries soon after a feeding, gas may be the problem. Prop the baby upright on your shoulder, and gently tap or rub the back. This may help bring up a burp that causes a tummy ache. Getting one burp may not be all that's needed.

Continue tapping until the baby stops crying. You can also help a baby release gas by placing him or her on your lap in a sitting position. Support the head and chin and tap or rub the back. (Remember gas can escape through either end, so listen for both sounds. Or wait for the baby's bowel movement, which may also relieve pain.)

You can also soothe a crying baby by carrying him or her around the room with a rocking motion.

Teeth on the Way

Teething can cause gum pain that makes a baby cry. Teething begins some time during a baby's first year. The timing is largely hereditary. As long as several weeks before the first tooth appears, the baby may gnaw on the fist or fingers. You may see a white spot on the gums.

The baby may be irritable and fussy, especially as the first tooth pushes against the gums. The pain may radiate to the jaw or ear. In response, the baby might rub the cheeks or pull on the ears. The baby may also have trouble sleeping.

A teething baby often drools, which may cause a rash on the chin. The excess saliva may also cause coughing or gagging. Babies put everything in their mouths, especially when teething, so keep dangerous items out of reach. The baby may also have a runny nose or a slight fever. (A high fever signals a more worrisome illness. Call a doctor.)

If you think your baby is crying because of teething, there are some steps you can take. Give the baby teething toys and rings. (Avoid toys with PVC or BPA, chemicals that can be poisonous.) Look for toys meant to be kept in the refrigerator or freezer until used. The cool temperature soothes sore mouths. You can also freeze a clean, wet washcloth for the baby to suck on. Frozen melon, peaches, or carrots are cold treats that also relieve inflammation (cut them small enough to prevent choking). You can also use a topical anesthetic gel or oral infant acetaminophen for pain.

Teething toys kept in the refrigerator or freezer can help relieve a baby's gum pain. Avoid toys that contain PVC or BPA. These chemicals are poisonous.

Other Discomfort

Babies sleep a lot. They often fall asleep on their own. But sometimes they cry or act fussy when they're tired. You may need to rock the baby to comfort and relax him or her. You can also walk around the room or push the baby in a stroller. Some parents resort to placing the baby in a car seat and going for a drive. Many babies are lulled to sleep by the motion of a motor vehicle.

Environmental factors can sometimes make a baby cry. In general, to be comfortable, most babies need the same temperature as the mother. If you need a sweater, put one on the baby, too. However, take care that the baby does not get overheated. Many mothers rely on feeling the baby's hands or feet. But feeling the baby's tummy is a more reliable measure of his or her temperature. Ann Peters, author of *Babycare: Everything You Need to Know*, says the best room temperature for a sleeping baby is 64 degrees Fahrenheit (18 degrees Celsius).

A dirty diaper can cause discomfort when urine or feces come in contact with the baby's skin. Be sure to keep the diaper area clean and immediately treat any diaper rash that develops with medication or over-the-counter cream or ointment.

What Is Colic?

Colic is marked by continuous, inconsolable crying. It lasts as long as three hours and usually appears three or

♀ YOUR BABY CAN SIGN

Months before babies can speak, they are well aware of their surroundings. They know what they want; they just don't know how to tell you. If you teach your baby (and yourself) some basic sign language, you'll give him or her a way to communicate with you. That will cut down on frustration for you both!

Babies as young as three months old can learn to sign using the same language developed for people with hearing disabilities. Many parents and other caregivers use and encourage signing for their children.

Look for books or Web sites with pictures to teach yourself some common signs. Then use fun, repetition, and encouragement to teach them to your child. As the baby masters several signs, continue to expand the vocabulary.

more days per week. It often begins at the same time of day or night.

Other signs include clenched fists and knees drawn up to the chest, which may indicate severe stomach pain. The baby may pass gas, again indicating stomach pain. The baby may appear stressed and have a red face. He or she may refuse to feed and have a hard time falling asleep or staying asleep.

According to Peters, about 20 percent of babies suffer from colic. It first appears between the ages of two to four weeks. It may last as long as three months, even longer. The causes may vary from baby to baby. Doctors don't yet know what the causes are.

Some possibilities include sensitivity to the environment, discomfort, dairy intolerance, or other reasons. A baby who is highly sensitive to the environment will also be sensitive to any changes in the environment. These include such factors as temperature, noise, amount of light, or even smell or taste. Discomfort may come from trapped gas. A bottle-fed baby may take in too much air along with the milk. Changing to a feeding system designed for babies with colic may ease the situation.

Dairy intolerance may be a problem, too. Some babies may react to proteins in dairy products. If the mother is breastfeeding, she may try avoiding dairy products to see if the colic subsides. If bottle-feeding, the mother can switch to a hypoallergenic formula to see if that helps. Another suspect is the sugar found in milk. Some babies have trouble processing the sugar, called lactose. Babies getting formula with iron may become constipated—another potential source of stomachache. Consult a pediatrician to rule out these possibilities.

Dealing with a colicky baby can be stressful for the mother, especially at night, depriving her of sleep. Some ways to deal with the crying baby include using a pacifier or giving the baby a gentle massage or a warm, relaxing bath.

Signs of Illness

A crying baby may indicate illness, especially if the crying is either weak or excessive. You may notice irritability or drowsiness. The baby may be reluctant to feed. But the first sign of illness often is a fever. The best place to check for

CAREFULLY READ INSTRUCTIONS FOR YOUR BABY'S THERMOMETER TO ENSURE AN ACCURATE READING. DIGITAL THERMOMETERS LIKE THIS ONE ARE EASY TO READ AND TEND TO BE SIMPLE TO USE.

fever is the back of the baby's neck. If it feels hotter than usual, use an underarm digital thermometer or digital ear thermometer. These are easy to use, but be sure to read the directions carefully to get an accurate reading. According to the Mayo Clinic, if the baby is younger than three months, call a doctor for any fever. If the baby is three months or older, contact a doctor if the oral temperature is 102°F (38.9°C) or higher.

Also look for other symptoms such as failure to smile, fewer wet or dirty diapers than usual, rash, vomiting, or diarrhea. Call a doctor, urgent care center, or hospital emergency room as warranted.

CHAPTER 7

Baby Care and Safety

The responsibility of taking care of an infant and keeping him or her safe can be overwhelming. Preparation, information, and education will ease the anxiety. Many childbirth classes include guidance for baby care. If not, ask your practitioner to help you find a parenting class.

Feeding the baby is the first priority. Experts agree that mother's milk is the best food for baby for the first year—or beyond. In fact, nursing for the first several days gives the infant the mother's immunities to illness through a substance called colostrum. Colostrum is the first breast milk produced. It contains antibodies that ward off disease.

Many women struggle with breastfeeding. If you don't choose to breastfeed or are unable to, commercial formula is available to bottle-feed the baby. Research has suggested that touching and the act of holding a baby during feeding may be what contributes most to the positive development of the baby, and you are absolutely able to do this

♀ PREPARE FOR EMERGENCIES

No one likes to think about worst-case scenarios. However, being prepared for them will help you deal with them if they occur.

Every new mother should know first-aid basics, as well as how to perform CPR. A first-aid class teaches how to respond to such situations as head injury, seizures, burns, poisoning, and other injuries or accidents. CPR clears an obstructed airway, restores breathing, and keeps oxygen flowing to the brain until emergency services arrive with more advanced life support.

Take the infant CPR class, especially for choking, which is more common among babies than heart attacks. As the baby grows, look for a child/adult class. Hospitals, the American Red Cross, the American Heart Association, as well as community groups and organizations offer these classes. You can also find them online. Take your first classes before the baby comes. Renew the certification every two years.

whether you're able to breastfeed or not. In both cases, milk is the most important part of an infant's diet. Babies should be fed when they're hungry (they'll let you know by acting fussy or crying). That may seem obvious. However, some new mothers try to put the baby on a feeding schedule. Just like you, an infant is hungry at different times and ready for different amounts of food throughout the day. "On demand" feeding is best for the baby and ensures a breastfeeding mother's milk supply will replenish itself for the next feeding.

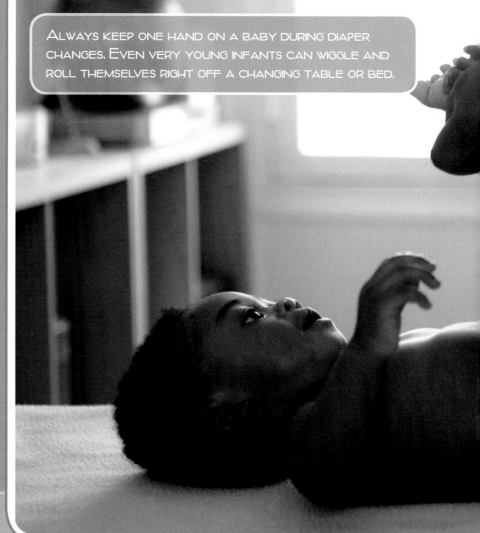

Around the six-month mark, you can introduce solid foods with the advice of the baby's doctor. It's important to give only one new food at a time. This helps in identifying food allergies or sensitivities.

CHANGING DIAPERS

Keeping the baby clean involves changing diapers and bathing him or her. Diaper changes are easy to do

ALWAYS KEEP ONE HAND ON A BABY DURING DIAPER CHANGES. EVEN VERY YOUNG INFANTS CAN WIGGLE AND ROLL THEMSELVES RIGHT OFF A CHANGING TABLE OR BED.

and usually not bad enough to gross you out. (If it is, take a deep breath and tough it out. You'll get used to it.)

Place the baby on a clean, wide surface and always keep one hand on her or him to prevent falls. Remove the dirty diaper. Use a damp washcloth or baby wipe to clean the entire bottom area. Wipe from front to back to help prevent urinary tract infections. An uncircumcised penis needs no special cleaning. Do not pull back the foreskin.

Look for signs of diaper rash on the skin and use a medicated cream or ointment as needed. Put a new diaper on the baby. Dispose of the dirty diaper and wipes. Wash your hands with soap.

BATHING BABIES

Bathing the baby keeps him or her clean. It also has the same relaxing effect that it has on older children and adults. Until the umbilical cord stump falls off in a week to ten days, you'll need to give sponge baths. The stump will fall off on its own, so keep it clean and dry until it does. (To ensure that the area heals, resist the urge to pull on it, even if it's hanging on by a thread!) After that, you can give baths in a sink, baby bathtub, or regular bathtub. Be sure the tub is cleaned first if it is shared by other family members.

Bathwater should be warm to the touch (test with your elbow or forearm). Just run a few inches of water in the bottom of the tub and place the baby in it. Use no-tears shampoo and soap designed for baby use. Try to keep the baby warm during the bath by pouring water over the skin from a plastic cup. As soon as you rinse, remove the baby from the water and wrap him or her in a warm towel. Diaper and dress the baby first. You can go back later to clean up the bath site. Always keep one hand in contact with the baby, and never leave him or her alone in a bath even for one single second. A baby can drown in a very small amount of water.

Bedtime Sleeping

When it's time for sleeping, place the infant on his or her back with the feet close to the foot of the crib. Be sure the crib sheet fits tightly. Remove any pillows, crib bumpers, stuffed animals, or dolls. Place the baby in a sleep sack or cover him or her with a small blanket tightly tucked under the foot of the crib mattress and pulled up only to the waist. This is the safest position. As babies grow and become able to roll over, they'll be able to reposition themselves for comfort without risking suffocation as long as the bed is otherwise clear.

Baby-Proof Your Home

While no house is 100 percent baby proof, you can take important steps to minimize the risk of injury and accident. Start with a smoke alarm on every level of your house. Check the batteries every time daylight saving time changes. Place lamps and other items at least 3 feet (1 meter) from the crib. Tie up all electrical cords, and keep the cords on blinds and shades out of reach. Install covers on all unused electrical sockets.

Prevent falls with baby gates at the top of staircases. Use childproof locks on all cupboards and cabinets the baby can reach. Also store all medicines, cleaning supplies, alcohol, and toiletries up high and locked away. Don't forget to secure garden chemicals and other items in the garage. Post phone numbers for poison control,

For family safety, install a working smoke alarm on every level of your residence. Check the batteries every time daylight saving time changes to make sure the alarm never stops working.

doctors, and emergency contact individuals in an easy-to-see location or load them into your mobile phone.

Water hazards like swimming pools (even wading pools in the backyard) and ponds pose significant danger. Be sure to keep fences and gates locked. For home swimming pools, install an alarm that alerts you to anything (or anyone) falling into the water. You can teach your baby swim safety skills beginning as early as you can give him or her a bath. Check with the American Red Cross or your community pool for lessons.

Who Will Watch the Baby?

Constant supervision is the best way to protect your child, especially outdoors. Never leave a child unattended at home or in public, especially in stores and parks. And never leave a child alone in a motor vehicle.

Be cautious about who babysits for you when you're away. Whether you're going to school or working, you may be able to leave the baby with a trusted relative or friend. Or you might need a nanny or in-home or center-based day-care provider. Many communities have referral organizations that will help you find appropriate day care. Be sure to ask for background checks on all individuals who will have contact with your baby. Also ask if the individual or staff are certified in first aid and cardiopulmonary resuscitation (CPR).

Once you start leaving your baby with someone, watch for signs that your child is being mistreated. If your

child becomes withdrawn or has changes in eating or sleeping habits, he or she may be reacting to the situation. If the child suddenly gets upset when left with the caregiver, you may want to reconsider your caregiver. (But remember that some children experience anxiety when their mother leaves, no matter who the caregiver is.)

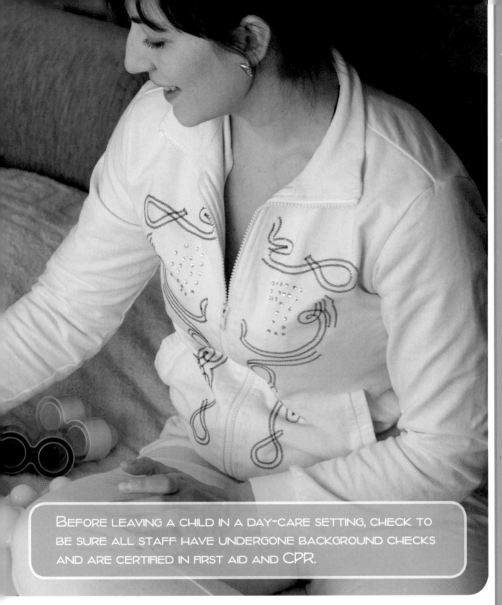

BEFORE LEAVING A CHILD IN A DAY-CARE SETTING, CHECK TO BE SURE ALL STAFF HAVE UNDERGONE BACKGROUND CHECKS AND ARE CERTIFIED IN FIRST AID AND CPR.

If you have any doubts, look for a different person to watch your child.

If someone is providing care in your own home, consider investing in a nanny cam, which is a hidden camera that records your nanny in action. You may also look for a system that lets you watch your baby live from your desk at work.

Helping Pets Adjust to the Newcomer

Dogs and cats can be sensitive to having a new person around—no matter how small. Cats usually have an easier time adjusting to the newcomer than dogs. Before introducing the baby, place a used blanket or piece of clothing with the baby's scent on it near a dog's bed or where a cat will find it. (If you're staying overnight in a hospital or birth center, ask a friend to do this for you before you come home.)

For either species, greet the pet alone, outside the baby's presence. Bring the baby in and let the animal sniff him or her. Look for opportunities to pet or play with your pet when the baby is sleeping. According to the American Society for the Prevention of Cruelty to Animals (ASPCA), there is "no truth to the myth that cats suck the air out of babies' lungs."

WHEN TO CALL THE BABY'S DOCTOR

If you think your baby is sick, you're probably right. Trust your instincts. The Mayo Clinic advises seeking emergency care for bleeding that can't be stopped; poisoning; seizures; trouble breathing; head injuries; sudden lack of energy or paralysis; unresponsiveness; large cuts or burns; neck stiffness; blood in urine or diarrhea; and skin or lips that look blue, purple, or gray.

However, cats may want to cuddle up with a sleeping child, which could be a smothering risk. Keep the cat out of the baby's sleeping room, and certainly out of the crib. Dogs, on the other hand, are pack animals. They want to be with you and the baby. So don't tie the dog outside or close him or her off in a separate room. The dog will come to protect the baby the same way he or she guards you.

ENJOYING MOTHERHOOD

Babies are not all work all the time, although it may sometimes seem so. Be sure to take the time to enjoy your infant. Cuddle the baby, or just hold him or her. The most important thing you can do is love your baby. The rest will come with time and practice.

anemia A low number of red blood cells that causes weakness, fatigue, pale skin, or shortness of breath.

birth plan A list of your preferences for what happens during and after labor and birth.

cervix The lower third of the uterus.

colic Continuous, inconsolable crying that lasts for hours and usually occurs about the same time of day or night three or more times per week.

colostrum The first breast milk produced around the time of birth. It contains antibodies that ward off disease.

contraction A periodic tightening and relaxing of the uterus.

dairy intolerance A reaction to proteins in dairy products.

doula A nonmedical person trained in providing physical and emotional support during pregnancy, labor, birth, and the postpartum period.

embryo A developing human from the time cells of a zygote start dividing until about eight weeks of growth.

fetus A developing human between eight weeks of gestation and birth.

gestation The amount of time a baby grows in the uterus.

human chorionic gonadotropin (HCG) The pregnancy hormone that pregnancy tests react to.

induction The use of drugs or medical procedures to start labor.

labor The birthing process.

lactose The carbohydrate (sugar) found in milk.

Lamaze A childbirth education method that includes a holistic view of childbirth as a natural and normal process.

ovulation The release of an egg from the ovary.

placenta The organ that connects a fetus to the wall of the uterus.

umbilical cord The cord that connects the placenta to the developing embryo or fetus.

uterus A hollow, pear-shaped organ in a female's lower abdomen.

zygote A fertilized egg.

American Pregnancy Association
1425 Greenway Drive, Suite 440
Irving, TX 75038
(972) 550-0140
E-mail: questions@americanpregnancy.org
Web site: http://www.americanpregnancy.org
The American Pregnancy Association promotes reproduc-
tive and pregnancy wellness. It offers a toll-fee helpline;
Web site and other forms of education, research,
advocacy, and community awareness.

Canadian Association of Family Resource Programs (FRP)
707–331 Cooper Street
Ottawa, ON K2P 0G5
Canada
(866) 637-7226
E-mail: info@frp.ca
Web site: http://www.frp.ca
The FRP is a Canadian association of programs that pro-
vide resources through leadership and consultation for
those who care for children and support families.

Canadian Association of Pregnancy Support Services
(CAPSS)
#304–4820 Gaetz Avenue
Red Deer, AB T4N 4A4

Canada
(866) 845-2151
Web site: http://www.capss.com
The CAPSS is a nonpolitical Christian charity that equips
  pregnancy support service centers across Canada.
  These centers provide practical, material, emotional,
  and spiritual help for families and women with distress-
  ing pregnancies.

International Childbirth Education Association (ICEA)
1500 Sunday Drive, Suite 102
Raleigh, NC 27607
(800) 624-4934
E-mail: info@icea.org
Web site: http://www.icea.org
The ICEA is a nonprofit professional organization. It provides
  training, educational resources, and professional certification programs for educators and health care providers
  who help women make decisions based on knowledge
  of alternatives in maternity and newborn care.

La Leche League International
P.O. Box 4079
Schaumburg, IL 60168-4079
(800) 525-3243
Web site: http://www.llli.org

La Leche League International supports and encourages
mothers to breastfeed. It provides mother-to-mother
information and education about the importance of
breastfeeding in infant nutrition and development.

National Campaign to Prevent Teen and Unplanned
Pregnancy
1776 Massachusetts Avenue NW, Suite 200
Washington, DC 20036
(202) 478-8500
Web site: http://www.thenationalcampaign.org
The National Campaign to Prevent Teen and Unplanned
Pregnancy is a private, nonpartisan organization that
seeks to prevent unplanned pregnancy, especially
among unmarried young adults.

National Healthy Mothers, Healthy Babies Coalition (HMHB)
2000 N. Beauregard Street, 6th Floor
Alexandria, VA 22311
(703) 837-4792
E-mail: info@hmhb.org
Web site: http://www.hmhb.org
The HMHB is an informal group of six lead organizations
to improve public and professional education about
prenatal and infant care, as well as improving the
health and safety of families, mothers, and babies.

Parents Without Partners, Inc.
1100-H Brandywine Boulevard
Zanesville, OH 43701-7303
(800) 637-7974
Web site: http://www.parentswithoutpartners.org
Parents Without Partners, Inc., is an international, nonprofit
    membership organization for single parents and their
    children. It provides educational and social activities
    that offer support, friendship, and exchange of parent-
    ing techniques. It also offers activities for children in
    single-parent families.

Planned Parenthood Federation of America
434 West 33rd Street
New York, NY 10001
(212) 541-7800
Web site: http://www.plannedparenthood.org
Planned Parenthood is a sexual and reproductive health
    care provider. It provides sex education and health care,
    and it advocates for reproductive health and rights.

Women, Infants, and Children (WIC)
U.S. Department of Agriculture
1400 Independence Avenue SW
Washington, DC 20250
(202) 720-2791

E-mail: wichq-web@vns.usda.gov

Web site: http://www.fns.usda.gov/wic

The WIC is a government program administered by the
U.S. Department of Agriculture through state agencies.
It provides food, information on healthy eating, and
referrals to health care for women, infants, and children
up to age five who are nutritionally at risk.

WEB SITES

Due to the changing nature of Internet links, Rosen
Publishing has developed an online list of Web sites
related to the subject of this book. This site is updated
regularly. Please use this link to access the list:

http://www.rosenlinks.com/WOM/Preg

Baratz-Logsted, Lauren. *Angel's Choice*. New York, NY: Simon Pulse, 2006.

Campbell, Carol P. *Frequently Asked Questions About Teen Pregnancy*. New York, NY: Rosen Publishing, 2011.

Carlson, Melody. *Anything But Normal*. Grand Rapids, MI: Revell, 2010.

Cupala, Holly. *Tell Me a Secret*. New York, NY: HarperTeen, 2010.

Curtis, Glade B. *Your Pregnancy Week by Week*. Cambridge, MA: Da Capo Press, 2011.

Deering, Kathryn. *A Little Book of Tweets for Moms*. Uhrichsville, OH: Barbour Publishing, 2012.

Frohnapfel-Krueger, Lisa. *Teen Pregnancy and Parenting*. Farmington Hills, MI: Greenhaven Press, 2010.

Iovine, Vicki. *The Girlfriends' Guide to Pregnancy*. New York, NY: Pocket Books, 2007.

Kern, Peggy. *The Test*. West Berlin, NJ: Townsend Press, 2010.

Knowles, Jo. *Jumping Off Swings*. Somerville, MA: Candlewick Press, 2009.

Lawton, Sandra. *Pregnancy Information for Teens: Health Tips About Teen Pregnancy and Teen Parenting*. Detroit, MI: Omnigraphics, 2007.

MacKay, Jenny. *Teen Pregnancy*. San Diego, CA: Lucent Books, 2011.

McDowell, Pamela. *Straight Talk About Teen Pregnancy*. New York, NY: Crabtree Publishing, 2010.

McGill, Elizabeth. *Pregnancy Information for Teens: Health Tips About Teen Pregnancy and Teen Parenting.* Detroit, MI: Omnigraphics, 2012.

Nolan, Han. *Pregnant Pause.* New York, NY: Harcourt Children's Books, 2011.

Retnasaba, Lila. *Baby Sign Language Official Reference Dictionary.* BabySignLanguage.com, 2011.

Riley, Laura. *You and Your Baby Pregnancy: The Ultimate Week-by-Week Pregnancy Guide.* Hoboken, NJ: Wiley, 2012.

Spock, Benjamin. *Dr. Spock's Baby and Child Care.* New York, NY: Gallery Books, 2012.

Williams, Heidi. *Teen Pregnancy.* Farmington Hills, MI: Greenhaven Press, 2009.

Willis, Laurie. *Teen Parenting.* Farmington Hills, MI: Greenhaven Press, 2011.

Alphonse, Lylah M. "Is Crying It Out Dangerous for Kids?" Shine from Yahoo!, December 16, 2011. Retrieved December 30, 2011 (http://shine.yahoo.com /parenting/crying-dangerous-kids-one-expert-says -222400379.html).

Bohn, Yvonne, Allison Hill, and Alane Park. *The Mommy Docs' Ultimate Guide to Pregnancy and Birth.* Cambridge, MA: Da Capo Press, 2011.

Contracept.com. "Understanding Your Risks." 2011. Retrieved December 29, 2011 (http://www.contracept .org/risks.php).

CoolNurse. "Teen Pregnancy." August 11, 2011. Retrieved December 18, 2011 (http://www .livestrong.com/article/12457-teen-pregnancy).

Dahl, Gordon B. "Early Teen Marriage and Future Poverty." *Demography*, Vol. 47, No. 3, August, 2010, pp. 689–718.

eDivorcePapers.com. "Teen Marriage and Divorce." Retrieved December 30, 2011 (http://www .edivorcepapers.com/marriage-and-divorce/teen -marriage-and-divorce.html).

Johnson, Melissa. "New Cesarean Guidelines: Will They Really Reduce the Rate of Repeat C-Sections?" *Everyday Health*, July 23, 2010. Retrieved January 2, 2012 (http://www.everydayhealth.com/blog/health -in-the-news/2010/07/23/new-cesarean-guidelines).

Kropp, Tori. *The Joy of Pregnancy*. Boston, MA: Harvard Common Press, 2008.

Landau, Erika, and Abigail Brenner. *The Essential Guide to Baby's First Year*. New York, NY: Alpha Books, 2011.

Lane, Brenda J., and Ilana T. Kirsch. *Pregnancy Guide: An Illustrated Handbook for Every Trimester*. Guilford, CT, 2009.

Leeds, Regina. *One Year to an Organized Life with Baby*. Cambridge, MA: Da Capo Press, 2011.

Mayo Clinic Staff. "Sick Baby? When to Seek Medical Attention." February 2, 2011. Retrieved December 27, 2011 (http://www.mayoclinic.com/health/healthy -baby/PR00022).

McKenna, James J. "Cosleeping and Biological Imperatives: Why Human Babies Do Not and Should Not Sleep Alone." Natural Child Project. Retrieved January 1, 2012 (http://www.naturalchild.org /james_mckenna/biological.html).

Peters, Ann. *Babycare: Everything You Need to Know*. New York, NY: Dorling Kindersley, 2011.

Retnasaba, Lila. *Baby Sign Language Comprehensive Teaching Guide*. BabySignLanguage.com, 2011.

Ricciotti, Hope, and Vincent Connelly. *I'm Pregnant! Now What Do I Eat?* New York, NY: Dorling Kindersley, 2007.

Stein, Rob. "Rise in Teenage Pregnancy Rate Spurs New Debate on Arresting It." *Washington Post*, January 26,

2010. Retrieved December 18, 2011 (http://www
.washingtonpost.com/wp-dyn/content/article/2010
/01/25/AR2010012503957_2.html).

Sutter Health. "Amniotic Fluid/Bag of Water." Retrieved
January 1, 2012 (http://www.babies.sutterhealth
.org/laboranddelivery/ld_am-flu.html).

Sutton, Amy L. *Pregnancy and Birth Sourcebook*. Detroit,
MI: Omnigraphics, 2009.

University of Maryland Children's Hospital. "Teenage
Pregnancy Rates Highest in the United States." May
10, 2011. Retrieved December 18, 2011 (http://
www.umm.edu/pediatreics/pregnancy.htm).

U.S. Consumer Product Safety Commission. "Crib Safety
Tips." Retrieved January 1, 2012 (http://www.cpsc
.gov/spscpub/pubs/5030.html).

WebMD. "Pregnancy and Conception." 2007. Retrieved
December 29, 2011 (http://www.webmd/com
/baby/guide/understanding-conception).

INDEX

A

abortion, 8, 18
abstinence, 10
adoption, 8
alcohol, 41, 59
amniotic fluid, 35, 38, 56, 74
anemia, 39, 50
anesthesia, 28
anticonvulsants, and pregnancy tests, 16
antihistamines, and pregnancy tests, 16
Apgar test, 71
aspirin, and pregnancy tests, 15
asthma, 50

B

baby names, 19
baby-proofing, 89–91
babysitters, 91–93
baby supplies, 54–59
bathing, 88
birth control pills, 10, 64
Birthing from Within, 26, 28
birth hypnosis, 26, 28
birthing coach, 28, 36–37
birth plans, 29–33, 36
bloody show, 67
bottle-feeding, 9, 82, 84–85
Bradley Method, 26, 28
breastfeeding, 9, 21, 28, 36, 38, 41, 54, 59, 69, 73, 77, 82, 84, 85
breast pump, 54

C

caffeine, 77
cardiopulmonary resuscitation (CPR), 85, 91
carpal tunnel syndrome, 46
car seats, 8, 63, 80
caul birth, 38
cervix, 48, 66, 68
cesarean sections, 28–29, 36, 64, 74
childbirth education, 8, 21, 25–28, 37
colic, 80–82
colostrum, 84
conception, process of, 12–13
condoms, 10
constipation, 44, 82
contraception, 7, 10
contractions, 3, 48, 56–57, 65, 66, 68, 69
co-sleeping, 59
counseling, 16–17, 20
cravings, 44
cribs, 8, 59, 61–62, 89, 95

D

day care, 21, 24, 91–93
depression, 21, 50
development, in the womb, 44–50
diabetes, 50, 51
diapers, 54–55, 80, 83, 86–88
diuretics, and pregnancy tests, 16

divorce, 18, 20
doctor
  finding, 33, 35–37
  questions to ask, 65
  when to call, 94
doula, 36
drugs, recreational, 41
due date, 42–43

E

eating disorders, 50
ectopic pregnancy, 51
education, completing while
    pregnant, 18–19, 20,
    22–24
eggs, 12, 51
embryo, 12, 44, 69
employment, 18–19, 21, 24
epilepsy, 50
exercise, 28, 40, 41–42, 64

F

fallopian tubes, 51
fatigue, 14, 46
feeding the baby, 8, 9, 31,
    76–78, 82, 84–86
fetus, 12, 44, 46, 48, 65,
    69, 74
fever, in infants, 78, 82–83
finances, 24
first-aid classes, 85
5-1-1 plan, 56–57
foster parenting, 8

G

galactosemia, 72
gas, 77, 82
General Educational
    Development (GED) test, 20

H

headache, 44, 51
heartburn, 44, 48
hemorrhoids, 48
hepatitis B virus, 72
high blood pressure, 50, 51
home births, 25, 29, 36
human chorionic gonadotropin
    (HCG), 12, 14, 16
humidifiers, 61

I

illness, signs of in babies,
    82–83
induced labor, 73–74

L

labor
  stage one, 66–68
  stage two, 68–69
  stage three, 69
  stage four, 69
lactose, 82
La Leche League, 21
Lamaze, 26, 27–28
liver problems, 46
low birth-weight babies, 40

M

marriage, 18–20
maternity clothes, 52–54
Medicaid, 25
medication, to relieve pain
    during birth, 25, 31, 36,
    68, 69
menstruation, 14, 43, 64
midwife, 35, 36, 57, 73
migraines, 50
miscarriage, 8, 14
mood swings, 14
morning sickness, 14, 46
movement, in the womb, 46, 48

N

nausea, 14, 46, 51
newborn health care, 71–72
nicotine, 41
nurse-midwife, 35
nursery, creating a, 61–62
nutrition, 8, 28, 40–41, 47

O

obesity, 50
online classes, 20, 22
ovaries, 12, 51
ovulation, 10, 12, 38

P

pets, 94–95
phenylketonuria, 72

placenta, 39, 69
preeclampsia, 51
pregnancy
    complications, 46, 50–51
    first trimester, 44
    myths and facts about, 38–39
    second trimester, 46, 48, 52
    statistics on teen, 6–7
    symptoms, 14–16
    telling your parents, 16, 17
    third trimester, 48–50
pregnancy test, 8, 14–16
premature infants, 41, 73
prenatal vitamin, 40, 47

S

sexually transmitted diseases, 10,
    50, 72
shotgun wedding, 18
sickle cell disease, 72
sign language, 81
single motherhood, 21
skin, darkening during preg-
    nancy, 46
sleep,
    options for the baby, 59–61, 80
    safe position for infants, 89
sleep sacks, 57
sperm, 12
stillbirths, 8
stretch marks, 46
sudden infant death
    syndrome, 64

T

teething, 78
terminal meconium, 35
thyroid disease, 50
  hypothyroidism, 72
tranquilizers, and pregnancy
    tests, 16

U

umbilical cord, 39, 72, 88
underwater birth, 25
urination, frequent, 14
uterus, 12, 16, 43, 48, 51, 65,
    66, 69
  tumors, 50

V

vitamin A, 41, 47
vitamin K, 72
vitamins, 40, 41, 47, 72

W

weight gain, 40, 44,
    46, 64
withdrawal method, 10
Women, Infants, and
    Children (WIC), 21

Z

zygote, 12

ABOUT THE AUTHOR

Mary-Lane Kamberg is a professional writer and speaker in Olathe, Kansas. One of her two daughters is a certified Bradley Method childbirth instructor.

PHOTO CREDITS

Cover, back cover, pp. 10, 25, 40, 52, 65, 75, 84 © iStockphoto.com/Reuben Schulz; pp. 6–7 © iStockphoto.com/Rosemarie Gearhart; p. 11 Medioimages/Photodisc/Thinkstock; pp. 12–13 Tinydevil/Shutterstock.com; pp. 14–15 Tyler Marshall/Getty Images; pp. 16–17 Purestock/Getty Images; pp. 22–23 © iStockphoto.com/Nathan Gleave; pp. 26–27 © Cindy Yamanaka/The Orange County Register/Zuma Press; pp. 30, 54–55 iStockphoto/Thinkstock; pp. 32–33 Thomas Northcut/Riser/Getty Images; p. 34 Oleksiy Maksymenko/All Canada Photos/Getty Images; pp. 42–43 Brand X Pictures/Thinkstock; p. 45 Ralph Hutchings/Visuals Unlimited/Getty Images; p. 49 Gwen Shockey/Photo Researchers, Inc.; p. 53 Iakov Filimonov/Shutterstock.com; p. 56 Andersen Ross/Blend Images/Getty Images; p. 58 © iStockphoto.com/Gene Chutka; p. 60 Keith Goldstein/Photographer's Choice/Getty Images; pp. 66–67 wavebreakmedia ltd/Shutterstock.com; p. 70 Tom Grill/Stone/Getty Images; p. 71 Frederick R McConnaughey/Photo Researchers/Getty Images; pp. 76–77 Shanta Giddens/Shutterstock.com; p. 79 Ross Whitaker/Stone/Getty Images; p. 83 Tina Rencelj/Shutterstock.com; pp. 86–87 Rayes/Lifesize/Thinkstock; p. 90 Jeffrey Coolidge/Iconica/Getty Images; pp. 92–93 Stokmen/Shutterstock.com.

Designer: Nicole Russo; Editor: Bethany Bryan; Photo Researcher: Karen Huang